Why Am I a Fish?

Greg Pyers

Chicago, Illinois

Typeset in 21/30 pt Goudy Sans Book
Printed and bound in China by South China
Printing Company Ltd

10 09 08 07 06
10 9 8 7 6 5 4 3 2 1

Library of Congress Cataloging-in-Publication Data
Pyers, Greg.
  Why am I a fish? / Greg Pyers.
    p. cm. -- (Classifying animals)
  Includes bibliographical references.
  ISBN 1-4109-2015-1 (library binding-hardcover) --
  ISBN 1-4109-2022-4 (pbk.)
  1. Fishes--Juvenile literature. I. Title.
  QL617.2.P94 2006
  597--dc22
                          2005012221

Acknowledgments
The author and publishers are grateful to the following for permission
to reproduce copyright material: Heather Angel/Natural Visions: p. **22**;
APL/Corbis/© Dale C. Spartas: p. **20**, /© Robert Pickett: pp. **21**, **23**;
Getty Images/National Geographic: p. **19**, /Photographer's Choice:
p. **26**; Ken Lucas/Visuals Unlimited: p. **12**; marinethemes.com/Kelvin
Aitken: pp. **8**, **15**, /Mark Conlin: p. **13**; Photolibrary.com: p. **16**,
/AnimalsAnimals: pp. **7**, **25**, /OSF: p. **9**; Photo Researchers, Inc./Nigel
Cattlin: p. **24**, /Roger Wilmhurst: p. **10**; Seapics.com/© Reinhard
Dirscherl: pp. **17–18**, /© Doug Perrine: pp. **4–6**; Silvestris Fotoservice/
ANTPhoto.com: p. **27**.

Cover photograph of a rainbow trout reproduced with permission
of Getty/Photographer's Choice.

Every effort has been made to contact copyright holders of any material
reproduced in this book. Any omissions will be rectified in subsequent
printings if notice is given to the publisher.

The paper used to print this book comes from sustainable resources.

Contents

Words that are printed in bold, **like this**, are explained in the glossary on page 31.

All Kinds of Animals

There are millions of different kinds of animals. There are spotted animals and striped animals. There are animals with eight legs and eight eyes. There are animals with no legs and no eyes. Some animals even look like plants!

But have you noticed that, despite all these differences, some animals are still rather similar to one another?

Clown fish are striped animals.

Sorting

Names in a phone book are sorted so that we can find the right number when we need it. Animals that are similar to one another can also be sorted into groups. Sorting animals into different groups can help us learn about them. This sorting is called **classification**.

This chart shows one way that we can sort animals into groups. Vertebrates are animals with backbones. Invertebrates are animals without backbones. Fish are vertebrates.

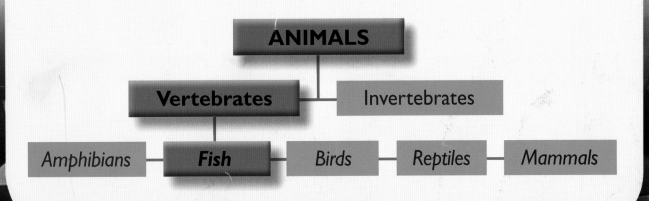

A Trout Is a Fish

Fish are one group of animals. There are more than 20,000 **species**, or kinds, of fish. Sea horses, manta rays, and eels are fish. So are rainbow trout. These animals all look very different from one another. So, what makes a fish a fish? In this book, we will look closely at the rainbow trout to find out.

As you read through this book, you will see a ✔ next to important information that tells you what makes a fish a fish.

A rainbow trout is a brightly colored fish.

6

Fresh water and salt water

✔ All fish live in water. River rainbow trout live only in cold fresh water, such as in mountain lakes and streams. Many other species of fish live in fresh water. There are also many species of fish that live only in the sea. These are called saltwater fish. Tuna, stingrays, and whale sharks are saltwater fish.

A sea dragon is a saltwater fish.

FAST FACT

The coastal rainbow trout, or steelhead, spends part of its life in the saltwater sea and part of its life in fresh water. Salmon and barramundi are two other kinds of fish that live in both fresh water and salt water.

A Trout's Body

When you think of a fish, do you think of an animal with a pointy body? A rainbow trout has a body like this. So do many other fish. This body shape is called a streamlined body shape. A streamlined body shape helps a trout move easily through water.

A rainbow trout's body shape helps it to swim.

Fins and scales

Like nearly every other **species** of fish, a rainbow trout has fins. The fins on the sides of its body are called **pectoral fins**, the fins on its back are called **dorsal fins**, and the fins at the end of its body are called tail fins. Most fish have scaly skin. A rainbow trout's **scales** are soft and shiny.

A rainbow trout's slippery scales are covered by **mucus** made by the skin. This protects the trout's skin from disease.

Inside a Trout

There is a skeleton inside a rainbow trout. Like most fish, a rainbow trout has a skeleton made of many bones. Muscles are attached to the skeleton. The muscles are covered by the trout's scaly skin.

Backbone

Running along the rainbow trout's back is a backbone. ✔ All fish have a backbone. The rainbow trout's backbone is made up of many tiny bones joined together. The backbone is very important because the trout's fin bones, tail bones, **skull**, and ribs are attached to it.

A fish has a skeleton inside its body.

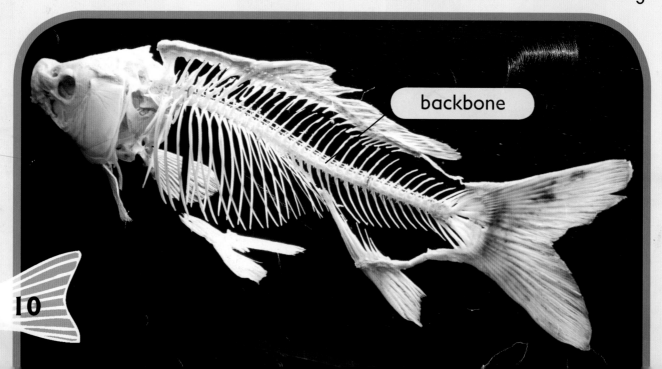

backbone

Organs

A rainbow trout has many **organs** in its body. Organs are body parts that have important jobs to do. For example, a rainbow trout's heart pumps blood around its body. Its brain sends messages to its muscles to make them work. Like most fish, a rainbow trout has no **lungs**.

brain gets messages from nostrils, eyes, and body and sends messages to muscles

These are some of the organs inside a rainbow trout.

heart pumps blood around body

stomach breaks down food

intestines pass **nutrients** into the blood

11

Gills

All living things need **oxygen** to survive. ✓ Like all fish, a rainbow trout has **gills** to take in oxygen from the water. A rainbow trout has two sets of gills, one on each side of the fish, just behind its head.

A rainbow trout often has a red patch on its gill cover.

gill cover

How gills work

As a rainbow trout swims along, it opens its mouth. Water moves into the mouth and passes out again through the gills. As the water moves through the gills, oxygen is taken into the blood. The blood then carries the oxygen around the trout's body. Rainbow trout cannot survive in water that has little oxygen. Cold water has the most oxygen in it. This is why rainbow trout live in cold mountain streams and lakes.

FAST FACT

A lungfish has gills and a **lung**. A lungfish gulps air into its lung when it cannot get enough oxygen from its gills. This happens when the water has very little oxygen in it.

A rainbow trout opens its mouth so that water can pass over its gills.

Moving

A rainbow trout moves by swinging the back half of its body from side to side. The tail fins sweep the water and push the fish along. The **pectoral fins** are used to change direction, stop, or stay in one place.

Swim bladder

Like many fish, a rainbow trout has an **organ** called a swim bladder. If the trout starts to sink, gas from its blood moves into the swim bladder and the fish stops sinking. If the trout starts to float, gas moves out of the swim bladder and the trout sinks.

FAST FACT

Sea horses are the only fish that swim upright. They beat their **dorsal fins** very fast to move forward.

swim bladder

Body temperature

Like most fish, a rainbow trout's body is the same **temperature** as the water it swims in. Some fish, such as the great white shark, can raise their body temperature. This helps the shark's muscles to work well even in very cold water.

The great white shark can hunt for **prey** in cold water.

15

Food

Rainbow trout eat many kinds of small animals. A rainbow trout's **diet** includes insects and their **larvae**, snails, leeches, crayfish, worms, and other fish. Sometimes rainbow trout eat the eggs of other fish. They also eat algae. Algae are simple **aquatic plants**.

Rainbow trout sometimes eat salmon eggs.

eggs

Teeth

Rainbow trout have small, sharp teeth on the upper part of their mouths. They are used for gripping **prey**. When the prey animal is caught, the trout swallows it whole. Most fish have teeth. The grass carp has small teeth for grinding plants. This fish also has teeth in its throat that grind the food before it reaches the stomach. A tiger shark has very sharp teeth for cutting through the flesh and bone of its prey.

A rainbow trout chases its prey and catches it in its mouth.

FAST FACT

The whale shark feeds on plankton. These are very tiny animals that drift on the ocean. The whale shark uses its **gills** like a strainer to take these tiny animals from the sea.

Senses

Like all fish, rainbow trout have senses to help them find food and stay away from **predators**. Their senses also help them to find each other and to find their way around.

Nostrils, lips, eyes, and ear

A rainbow trout has nostrils at the front of its head. These sense food smells in the water. It also has a sense of taste on its lips and large eyes for seeing under water. A rainbow trout can sense sounds with its ear. This is inside the fish's head.

A rainbow trout has one eye on each side of its head, giving it a good all-around view.

Lateral line

Along each side of a rainbow trout's body is the lateral line. Most fish have lateral lines. These lines help the fish to sense water movements. With its lateral lines, a rainbow trout can tell which way water is flowing in a stream.

FAST FACT

When an animal moves, its muscles give off tiny amounts of electricity. A shark's head has an electrosense. This sense picks up the electricity fish give off as they move. With this sense, a shark can find its **prey**, even when the shark cannot see it.

A rainbow trout's lateral line helps it to sense other fish swimming nearby.

lateral line

Eggs

Different fish have different life cycles. A female rainbow trout digs out a shallow hole in the gravel at the bottom of a stream in spring or summer. She lays up to 8,000 eggs in the hole. A male rainbow trout **fertilizes** the eggs. The eggs are then covered with gravel. The male and female trout will not return to care for the eggs.

A female rainbow trout finds a sheltered place to lay her eggs.

FAST FACT

Most **species** of fish begin their lives inside an egg, but gray nurse sharks give birth to live "pups."

Growing

A tiny rainbow trout begins to grow inside each egg. At this stage, it is called an **embryo**. How fast the embryos grow depends on the water **temperature**. If the water is warm, the embryos grow fast. They take longer to grow if the water is cold.

Protection

Rainbow trout eggs do not have a shell. They have a tough skin that protects the embryos from damage by the gravel. The skin is also a little sticky. This keeps the eggs from being washed away by the stream.

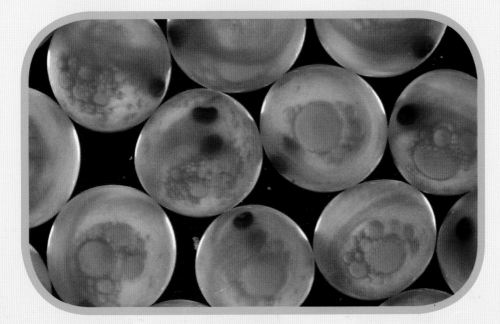

You can see rainbow trout embryos growing inside their eggs.

Young Fish

A rainbow trout's eggs usually begin to hatch six to eight weeks after being laid. The tiny rainbow trout break out of their eggs. But they do not swim away. Instead, they stay in the gravel. There, they are protected from being swept away by the stream or from being eaten by **predators**.

Newly hatched rainbow trout hide from predators among the gravel.

FAST FACT

Female sea horses are fish that lay their eggs in a pouch on the belly of a male sea horse. A few weeks later, the eggs hatch and the young sea horses leave to take care of themselves.

Food

The young fish survive on their yolk sacs, which are attached to their bodies. The yolk is the food from inside the eggs. After about three more weeks, the yolk is all used up. The young fish come out of the gravel.

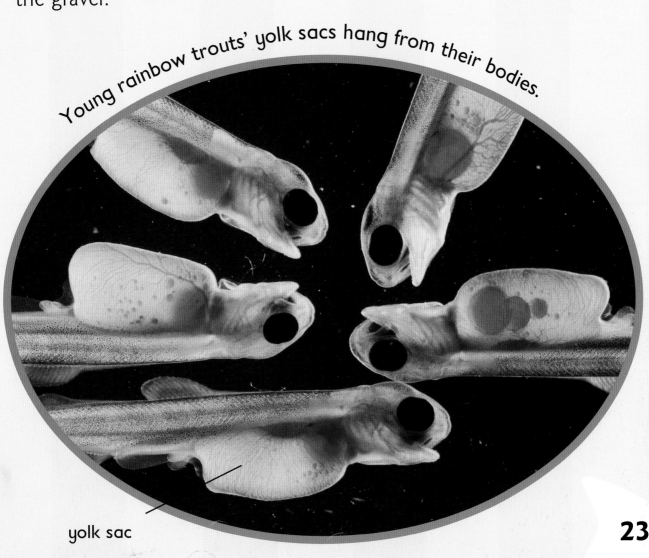

Young rainbow trouts' yolk sacs hang from their bodies.

yolk sac

Growing Up

With no parents to take care of them, the tiny rainbow trout keep together. At this stage in their lives they are called fry. They take shelter along the edge of the stream or lake. The fry are only about 1 to 2 inches (2.5 to 5 centimeters) long. This means they can eat only small **prey**, such as insects. They also eat **aquatic plants**.

As the rainbow trout fry grow, they begin to look more like **adult** rainbow trout.

Becoming adults

Very few young rainbow trout survive to become adults. Most will be eaten by **predators**, including other fish and birds. This is one reason why the female rainbow trout lays so many eggs. The rainbow trout fry stay in sheltered areas for two or three years. They move into the open water of lakes and streams when they are large enough to protect themselves.

Rainbow trout usually live six or seven years, but they can live much longer.

The great blue heron eats rainbow trout.

FAST FACT

In 2003 an Australian lungfish was still alive and well at 65 years old. This is the oldest known age for a fish.

Is It a Fish?

A rainbow trout is a fish, because:

- ✔ It has a backbone
- ✔ It has **gills**
- ✔ It lives in water
- ✔ Its body may be warm or cool, depending on its surroundings.

Rainbow trout are fish.

Test yourself: mudskipper

Mudskippers live in the sea. They come out of the water to hunt for worms and insects in the mud. They use their **pectoral fins** to pull themselves forward. Before a mudskipper leaves the sea, it takes a mouthful of water and closes its gills. While on land, the gills take in **oxygen** from this water. A mudskipper has a backbone and a slimy body. It lives in warm seas because it cannot make its own body heat.

Is the mudskipper a fish? You decide. (You will find the answer at the bottom of page 30.)

A mudskipper's eyes sit high so that it can see behind, forward, and to the sides.

Animal Groups

This table shows the main features of the animals in each animal group.

Mammals	Birds	Reptiles
backbone	backbone	backbone
skeleton inside body	skeleton inside body	skeleton inside body
most have four limbs	four limbs	most have four limbs
breathe air with **lungs**	breathe air with lungs	breathe air with lungs
most have hair or fur	all have feathers	all have **scales**
most born live; three **species** hatch from eggs; females' bodies make milk to feed young	all hatch from eggs with hard shells	many hatch from eggs with leathery shells; many born live
steady, warm body **temperature**	steady, warm body temperature	changing body temperature

![Fish] Fish	![Amphibians] Amphibians	![Insects] Insects
backbone	backbone	no backbone
skeleton inside body	skeleton inside body	exoskeleton outside body
most have fins	most have four limbs	six legs
all have **gills**	gills during first stage; **adults** breathe air with lungs	breathe air but have no lungs
most have scales	no feathers, scales, or hair	many have some hair
most hatch from eggs; some born live	all hatch from eggs without shells	many hatch from eggs; many born live
changing body temperature	changing body temperature	changing body temperature

Find Out for Yourself

Rainbow trout come from the streams and lakes of western Canada and the United States. For many years, they have been put into streams and lakes in many other parts of the world, including Great Britain and Australia. Rainbow trout are among the favorite fish of many fishermen, who catch them to eat.

You could buy a rainbow trout from a fish market and examine it carefully. You could look at its **gills** and fins, see how its mouth opens, and feel its skin and **scales**.

For more information about rainbow trout and other fish, you can read more books and look on the Internet.

More books to read

Lundblad, Kristina, and Bobbie Kalman. *Animals Called Fish*. New York: Crabtree, 2005.

Savage, Stephen. *Fish: What's the Difference?* Chicago: Raintree, 2000.

Using the Internet

You can explore the Internet to find out more about fish. An adult can help you use a search engine. Type in a keyword such as *fish* or the name of a particular fish **species**.

Answer to "Test yourself" question:
The mudskipper is a fish.

Glossary

adult grown-up

aquatic plant plant that lives in water

classification sorting things into groups

diet what an animal eats

dorsal fin fin on a fish's back

embryo very early stage in the growth of a fish inside its egg

fertilize make an embryo grow inside an egg

gills organs that take in oxygen under water

larva (more than one are called larvae) first stage in the life of some insects

lungs organs that take in air

mucus slimy liquid that protects a fish's skin

nutrient part of food that an animal needs to survive

organ part of an animal's body that has a certain task or tasks

oxygen gas that living things need to survive

pectoral fin fin on the side of a fish, near its head

predator animal that kills and eats other animals

prey animals that are eaten by other animals

scales pieces of thin, hard material that cover the bodies of most fish

skull all the bones of an animal's head

species kind of animal

temperature how warm or cold something is

Index